D-DAY
POOLE

DEREK BEAMISH AND IAN ANDREWS

POOLE HISTORICAL TRUST

The primary aims of Poole Historical Trust are the promotion of research into and the publication of works on the history and life of Poole and the surrounding areas.

PREVIOUS PUBLICATIONS
Pride of Poole
An Album of Old Poole
Mansions and Merchants of Poole and Dorset
Brownsea Islander
Poole and World War II
Portfolio of Old Poole
Ebb Tide at Poole
History of the Town of Poole, 1839 (reprint)
The Sydenhams of Poole
Art in Poole and Dorset
Victorian Poole
Poole after World War II 1945-1953

© Ian Andrews, 1993

ISBN 1 873535 10 4

Printed by Dolphin Printers (Poole)

ACKNOWLEDGEMENTS

D-DAY: POOLE was first published by Poole Tourism Service
in 1984.

Since that time more information has come to hand but sadly the
author, Derek Beamish, has died.

This booklet is published by Poole Historical Trust as a tribute to
Derek, who was a founder Trustee and its former Hon. Secretary.

The revisions have been made by Ian Andrews, M.A. (Oxon),
Honorary Borough Archivist and the current Honorary Secretary to
Poole Historical Trust.

*Many individuals and organisations have assisted in supplying material,
especially:*

Mrs Hazel Morton

Mrs C. Holmes

Miss M. England

Mr R. Bullen

Mr G. Goard

Mr W. Rose

(ex members of the 86 Field Regiment, Hertfordshire Yeomanry,
Royal Artillery)

Leading Seaman Lucas

Poole Historical Trust

Poole Museum Service

Poole Borough Archives (gift of Mrs Mair Beamish)

Poole Tourism Service

Poole Reference Library

Public Record Office

Department of the U.S. Navy Historical Centre.

Design by Graham Smith and Andrew Arnold
Additional photography Stephen Courtney

*POOLE AND WORLD WAR II, by Derek Beamish, Harold Bennett and
John Hillier, published by Poole Historical Trust in 1980 (now out of print)
told the full story of Poole in World War II.*

OPERATION NEPTUNE:D-1

In the early hours of Monday, 5th June 1944, a procession of 81 landing craft and launches made its careful way out of Poole Harbour. Once in the Bay the craft moved into 4 columns, each of the larger vessels taking one of the smaller craft in tow. A fresh south-westerly wind roughened the dark sea. Headed by 6 motor gun boats, the 4 long columns steered out into the Channel. Assault Convoy 02A had left its base for Omaha Beach in Normandy.

URGENT PREPARATIONS MUST BE MADE...

Long before that June morning Poole had played a vital part in the development of amphibious warfare and combined operations in World War II. As early as 1941 one of the very first Commando units had used the vast harbour as its training base before launching daring raids on the Channel Islands. In the following year, *Operation Sledgehammer*, one of the earliest plans for a full scale attack on Hitler's Europe, had resulted in the building of a large amphibious warfare centre in Hamworthy, *HMS Turtle*. Eventually holding over 4,000 personnel, this base, included the camp at Lake with a wide tank 'hard', Round Island and the Shaftesbury Homes in Constitution Hill Road. It specialised in training the crews of the gun ships and rocket firing landing craft which would support the troops landing on the beaches of France. The Royal Navy and Royal Marines practised with the Army on the nearby beach at Studland. Early in 1943 the D.D. (Amphibious) tanks held their first major exercise there. Headed by King George VI, a large gathering of senior commanders, including Lord Louis Mountbatten, the Chief of Combined Operations, and Generals Montgomery and Eisenhower, watched the hail of rockets and shells pouring down on the beach as the swimming tanks led in the first wave of the assault.

Poole shipyards built many of the craft, motor gun boats and launches for use in the invasion.

The British Power Boat Co. in West Quay Road was responsible for the Scott Paine designed motor gun boats. J. Bolson & Son employed 800 people and built launches, landing craft (at the rate of one a day) and minesweepers. More launches came from the Dorset Yacht Co. and R.A. Newman's in Hamworthy. From 1942 onwards many other landing craft crowded into the harbour for maintenance and repair in these yards. As D-Day came nearer their work became so urgent that restricted lighting was allowed to break the blackout and enable work to go on round the clock. J.R.Smith (Engineers) were working throughout the period to produce the parts for the Bailey Bridges that would be needed.

Deception played a large part in the invasion plans and a secret operation, codenamed *BIGBOX*, took place in July and August of 1943. The idea was to simulate a movement of landing craft from the west to the east of England. Dummy craft were rigged up from oil drums, scaffold poles and rolls of hessian and launched under cover of darkness, hoping they would be spotted by enemy reconnaissance aircraft in daylight. They were then dismantled and transported to another destination. An American unit was responsible for Cornwall and Devon and the members of the Pioneer Corps of 24 Airfield Construction Group R.E. took care of Poole, Bucklers Hard and West Wittering. About 12 skeleton craft were constructed at a time on the shingle of *HMS*

Churchill reviewing a training exercise in Wareham Forest.

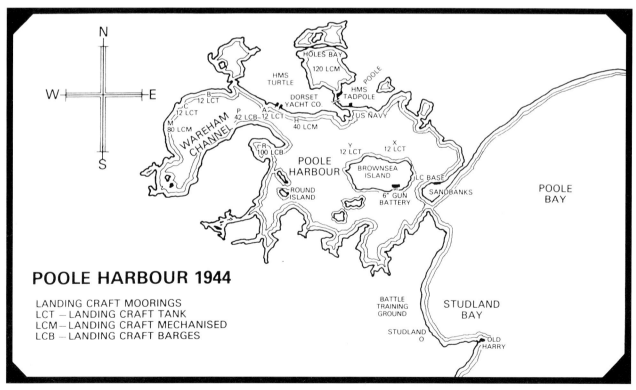

POOLE HARBOUR 1944

LANDING CRAFT MOORINGS
LCT – LANDING CRAFT TANK
LCM – LANDING CRAFT MECHANISED
LCB – LANDING CRAFT BARGES

Plan of Poole Harbour, 1944.

Pluto experiments in Poole Bay in March 1944. HMS Conundrum 1, underway.

Turtle, to be floated by the Royal Navy to the Hamworthy end of Brownsea Island. There they remained for 2 or 3 weeks before a similar number appeared at Bucklers Hard as the ones at Poole 'disappeared'. The currents in Poole Harbour caused some problems as they led to the flimsy craft appearing to have 'bends' in them! One night more boats had been rigged up than could be launched before daybreak and there was feverish activity to dismantle the surplus!

Another experimental exercise involved connecting Poole Quay to Brownsea Island by lengths of pipeline (helped by a local plumber, W.S. Rigler, later to become a Freeman of Poole) to test the feasibility of P.L.U.T.O. (Pipe Line Under The Ocean). After initial success, drums, known as *Conundrums*, were tested in Poole Bay and ultimately between the Bay and the Isle of Wight As a result a permanent station was constructed at Sandown from which vital petrol supplies could be pumped across the Channel.

ALL FORCE G UNITS WILL MOVE...

Up until January 1944 Poole was to be one of the main bases for the British invasion forces. Force G, assaulting Gold Beach, was to be launched from the Dorset ports. Then, when Montgomery insisted that the invasion front should be widened, the main facilities in Poole were allocated to the American troops who would attack over the Omaha and Utah beaches. But Force G, including the 1st Battalion of the Dorsetshire Regiment, the East Yorkshire and the Green Howards, needed to stay as long as possible in the Poole area to make use of the battle practice grounds there. They did not leave until 1944.

Veterans of another unit, the 86 Field Regiment, Hertfordshire Yeomanry, R.A., remember their days in Poole very clearly. Leaving their tented camps in Hamworthy Park and Rockley, they drove their Ram self-propelled guns onto tank landing craft at *HMS Turtle*. Sweeping out into Studland Bay, they turned for the beach, firing their 25 pounders as they stormed in to cover the landing of the troops. Other exercises used Brownsea Island and at least one steel helmet accidentally dropped into the water must still lie in the Harbour mud! After these last rehearsals 86 Regiment took their guns to the Alumhurst Road district in Bournemouth. Here they waterproofed their equipment before moving off to a sealed camp in woods near Romsey, waiting for their journey to Southampton and Normandy.

UNITED STATES FORCES ARE READY TO DEPLOY IN THE POOLE AREA...

Well before the British troops left, the Americans moved in. The U.S. Infantry 1st Division set up its headquarters under General Bradley in Langton House, near Blandford, in October 1943. 'The Fighting First', known as the 'Big Red One' from its distinctive badge, included many veterans of the landings in North Africa and Sicily. They were to be joined in the battle for Omaha Beach by men of the U.S. 29th Division, the 'Blue and Grey' and the 2nd and 5th Ranger Battalions, the American Commandos. These troops moved into tented camps in the Dorchester area. Another American force took over the fine Elizabethan mansion at Breamore. General Patton was to make it his headquarters.

The Americans soon made their mark on Poole and the surrounding district. Their engineers built 22nd General Hospital at Blandford and a large petrol depot at West Moors. Two more hospitals went up at St. Leonards, near Ringwood, to cater for up to 10,000 expected casualties, and at Shaftesbury. The 2nd Ranger Battalion who had the difficult task of scaling the 100 feet high cliffs at Pointe du Hoc to destroy a menacing battery of 6 German guns, moved into Langton Matravers. They rehearsed by climbing the cliffs at Swanage from their British assault craft. The 58th Army Field Artillery Battalion moved into Charborough Park (where, incidentally, the Borough Archives had been moved for safety and suffered more damage from damp and vermin than in the previous 500 years).

More and more GI's moved into Poole, taking over requisitioned halls, hotels and private houses. Denby Lodge in Fernside Road became a cookhouse where they collected their 'chow'. Out on the Canford Heath battle ground the 297 Engineer Combat Battalion perfected their mortar firing so enthusiastically that they cracked the walls and ceilings of many buildings in the Alderney District. Waste land off Herbert Avenue was used as a temporary supply base to store tanks and D.U.K.W.S., the amphibious lorries which would ferry guns and supplies from ship to shore in the invasion. (D was the year of origin (the 4th of the war); U = utility; K = front wheel drive; W = six wheeled).

Many of the GI's were billeted in Poole homes. When they had arrived in the country they had been warned that the British were "rather a shy sort". However, it was not long before the friendliness and generosity of the Americans broke down the reserve of the British people. In any case, the British were glad to see the GI's and only too aware of the sacrifices they would make for the common cause. Chance meetings in pubs, dance halls, churches and chapels, and impromptu baseball games in roads like Penn Hill Avenue led to firm friendships and many American servicemen became welcome guests in Poole homes.

MAXIMUM USE WILL BE MADE OF POOLE HARBOUR...

Naturally it was the quayside and harbour which saw the busiest activity. Early in 1944 the U.S. Army Transportation Corps arrived in Poole. Making their headquarters in Hill Street, they took over the quayside from the end of High Street to the Fisherman's Dock, as well as Hamworthy Quay. Black military policemen guarded the approaches to these areas where stockpiles of ammunition, fuel, chemical warfare material and rations were made ready. In May the U.S. Navy commissioned Poole as one of its advanced amphibious bases. Commander W.L. McDonald arrived with 800 men and 60 83ft coastguard cutters of No. 1. Rescue Flotilla, known as the 'matchbox fleet'. They were serviced at the old Slade warehouse near the Quay and they would accompany the invasion convoys as sea rescue craft. The U.S. Navy was also responsible for a growing collection of 240 landing craft in Poole. The American personnel, nearly 1,500 strong, moved into the huts at *HMS Turtle*,

while the Royal Navy crews were transferred to tented accommodation in the camp.

The Dorset Yacht Club became the American operational headquarters and other requisitioned property nearby accommodated specialist officers - the American engineers shared 'Windwhistle', No 59 Lake Drive with their R.N. counterparts. The showrooms of Carter's Pottery on Poole Quay, recently vacated by B.O.A.C. became the base administrative offices, while a dispensary was set up in the Shaftesbury Homes 'in Poole City' as the Americans called it. The Americans also took over Wood's Coalyard on the Quay from the Royal Navy.

Finding room to moor and maintain the British and American landing craft visiting or stationed in Poole had long been a problem both for the Naval Officer in charge of Poole and the captain of *HMS Turtle*. The situation was eased by the transfer from Poole of the flying boats belonging to 210 Squadron, R.A.F. Coastal Command and B.O.A.C. The smaller landing craft were maintained at the Dorset Yacht Co., Newman's and Bolson's yards and the former R.N.A.S. base at Sandbanks. Some of the larger craft were serviced up the Wareham River at Ridge. Others used May and Hassell's Yard by the Hamworthy Bridge. When this became full, Sydenham's Yard, then *HMS Tadpole*, a R.N. coastal force base, was also pressed into service. Over 500 landing craft were moored at 'trots' in the mouth of the Wareham River, off Brownsea Island and in Holes Bay. The U.S. coastguard cutters lay 8 deep along the Town Quay.

Slade's old Warehouse and yard on the Quay, first used by the Royal Navy, was taken over by the US Navy for their Coastguard Cutters in May 1944.

LCA's (Landing Craft Assault) built by Bolson, moored in Holes Bay. These wooden craft carried 35 troops

Landing craft at Dorset Lake Shipyards.

The success of the preparations for D-Day depended on maximum co-operation between the British and American forces. *HMS Turtle* was to supply 1200 men to crew landing craft for the attacks on Omaha and Utah and the follow-up service. The Americans needed to practice their navigation and gunnery. It was up to the British to provide a myriad of facilities for the invasion forces. A well camouflaged petrol dump was built in Poole Park and connected by pipe line to the Town Quay. More petrol and diesel was made ready on barges moored off New Quay and Hamworthy. A prisoner of war stockade was put up at *HMS Turtle*. Kits of clothing and personal necessities such as toothbrushes were made ready for survivors there, in the Poole Naval Headquarters above the National Westminster Bank in the Corn Market and the R.N. Victualling Store in Lagland Street. (For British survivors extra rum was set aside and with rare official generosity it was stated that "reports of such issues are not required.")

The operational orders for D-Day, running into thousands of pages, each stamped with a new copy security code *BIGOT*, left no detail untouched. Ten air-sea rescue launches, operating in pairs, were made ready in Poole for maximum effort on D-Day. They were under strict orders to return to base only when they were full, or survivors they had rescued were in need of urgent medical attention. The harbour authorities had to find room for 16 British minesweepers which would help clear the way for the invasion convoys. Two Post Office barges also waited in Poole, ready to lay telephone cables from a point in Tuckton to Normandy when the beachheads had been secured. Amongst the many young servicemen who were assembling in Poole a number of older men stood out in contrasting uniforms. These were Royal Observer Corps men from the depot in

Bournemouth who were to join the landing craft as aircraft spotters. Others were Merchant Navy men who had volunteered to join the D.E.M.S. and would also sail in the invasion fleet.

There was every danger that the convoys of landing craft, the camps and supply dumps, and the heavy rail and road traffic would be seen and attacked by the enemy navy and air force. The time of greatest danger was thought to be in April - May when the Germans would be bound to notice the concentration of forces and the movement of Force G from the Poole district. To counter the threat from the enemy 'E' boats the R.N. increased its offensive sweeps along the French coast. *HMS Tadpole's* 2 flotillas of gunboats joined in these operations. Poole already had 72 anti-aircraft guns to protect it but another 12 heavy weapons and 20 light guns were ordered into the district. Some of these extra guns were mounted on the roofs of high buildings such as the Cooperative offices in Longfleet Road and Marks and Spencers in High Street. The fighter aircraft now crowding the local airfields were another line of defence. R.A.F. Typhoons flew from Holmsley South and Hurn, with Mosquitos of the Royal Canadian Air Force, including the 125 (Newfoundland) Squadron, an appropriate duty for men in the Squadron who had old family connections with Poole. American Thunderbolts moved into Beaulieu, Christchurch, Ibsley and temporary airfields at Lymington, Winkton and Bisterne, near Ringwood. Six U.S.A.F. Lightning squadrons were based at Warmwell and at Stoney Cross in the New Forest.

Despite all precautions enemy aircraft were able to break through at night. In the early morning of 24th April, 70 bombers ranged over the Dorset area. Showers of incendiaries and a few bombs rained down on Poole and the Holton Heath area. They did little damage but 3 Poole people were killed. At the same time about 30 mines were dropped in Poole Bay. Most of them exploded when they hit the water and caused little interference to the invasion preparations.

(Above) Packed stem to stern, in some cases five deep, these US Coastguard Cutters line the quayside at Poole in 1944.

(Right) Plan of HMS Turtle, drawn from memory by a Wren.

(Below) Plan of Poole Quay and the Old Town, 1944.

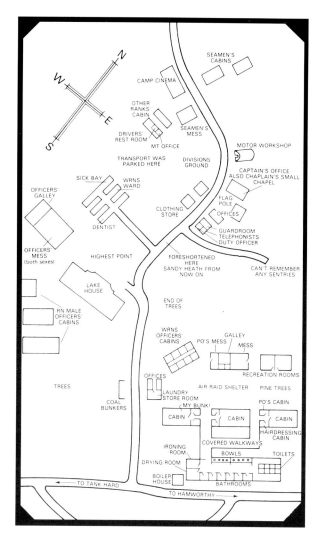

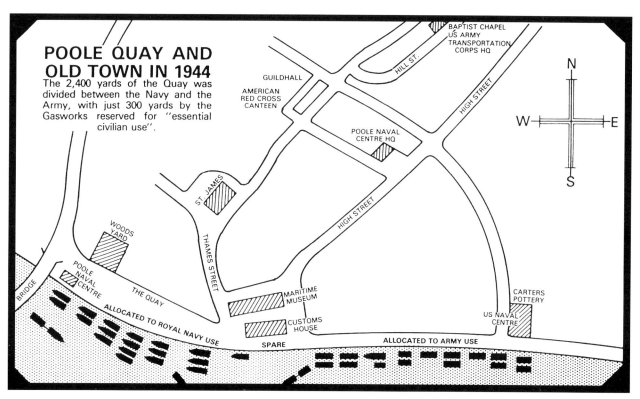

POOLE QUAY AND OLD TOWN IN 1944
The 2,400 yards of the Quay was divided between the Navy and the Army, with just 300 yards by the Gasworks reserved for "essential civilian use".

PROTECTED AREA NO.3: DORSET, THE BOROUGH OF POOLE

The date of D-Day and the exact point of the assault on France was still a closely guarded secret. Nevertheless the movement and gathering of landing craft, troops, vehicles and supplies made it obvious to all that some great venture was at hand. People also had a clue from the intensive security measures now being taken.

Poole became part of a 'Protected Area' along the south coast and movement into the district was carefully checked. Policemen boarded trains at Basingstoke to make sure that those travelling to the coast had a good reason for their journey. More and more people were stopped in the streets of Poole and asked to produce their identity cards. Quite a number had forgotten to carry them and were fined sums ranging from 2/6d (12 ½p) to 7/7d (38p) for their carelessness. The police were also busy visiting householders along the roads where military convoys stopped. They told them they must on no account post letters or make telephone calls for the servicemen in these convoys, in case some vital secrets were betrayed. On 1st May Poole Council agreed to the use of Wesley Hall as a rest centre for the growing number of American troops. Something was known to be up when, from 15th May, the sailing and boating permits of the local Sea Scouts were withdrawn.

At last, early in May, the roads grew quieter. The invasion troops were in sealed camps where they learnt the details of their part in the invasion plans. Only very exceptionally were they allowed out; segregated hospital accommodation was made ready for any who needed it. Then, at the end of the month, the roads were crowded once again as long convoys made their way to the quayside.

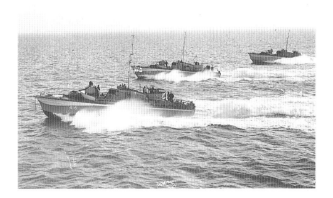

Motor Torpedo Boats returning just after dawn from anti-'E'-boat patrol off Cherbourg.

The Custom House and Quay, a protected area.

At the tank 'hard' *HMS Turtle*, Sherman tanks, bulldozers and half-track vehicles were driven on board 8 landing craft. The tanks, belonging to 'A' Company of the U.S. 743 Tank Battalion, were to form part of the Close Gunfire Support Group at Omaha Beach. Waiting for them to complete their loading were 5 landing craft equipped with heavy guns, 9 rocket armed craft and 7 vessels bristling with anti-aircraft guns. The many radio masts and aerials on another landing craft marked it out as the floating headquarters of this group. British officers stood on the bridges of these landing craft. They had trained the American crews and were to sail with them to Normandy. The orders issued by the Commanding Officer of Convoy 02A, Captain L.S. Sabin, left no room for misunderstanding. "The assault will be pressed home regardless of loss or difficulty... no vessel under my command will turn back

once the movement to the far shore is started. Breakdowns must be repaired at sea and the convoy rejoined as soon as possible. If it is not possible to overtake the convoy, head for the assault area." The gun craft were to open fire at specific targets such as pill-boxes precisely 20 minutes before the first wave of the assault reached the beach. Four minutes later, the Sherman tanks were to start firing from their landing craft. Just ten minutes before the first 'swimming' tanks led in the troops, the rocket craft were to launch their missiles at the enemy.

Another 20 smaller landing craft were also loaded for this assault convoy. They carried lorries and heavy equipment such as cranes and winches, as well as explosives. Some of these craft were allocated to demolition teams who had the dangerous and difficult task of

Some of the many Sherman Tanks that were stored in the area prior to D-Day.

blowing gaps in the lines of obstacles protecting the invasion beaches. Others were ready to make running repairs to landing craft. Ready to escort the convoy were 15 Coastguard rescue craft, 9 R.A.F. seaplane tenders, 4 American patrol craft and 2 R.N. motor launches which would act as navigation leaders.

There was no pause in the bustle at the tank 'hard' and quayside once the Omaha convoy had been loaded. Another four R.N. Convoys, of over 400 vessels, had to be made ready, two each would leave for Omaha (04 & 05) and Utah (U5 & U6) beaches. Some were fuelling trawlers, others were landing craft with additional repair equipment. Many were powered barges carrying large tanks of oil or

water or shrouded cargoes of ammunition. There were even two floating kitchens to supply hot meals to the invasion forces, or make smoke to protect the off-shore craft from enemy attack. Out in the Bay, U.S. destroyers waited to escort these convoys across the Channel.

US Coast Guard Cutters No.2, 4, and 29 moored at Poole Quay.

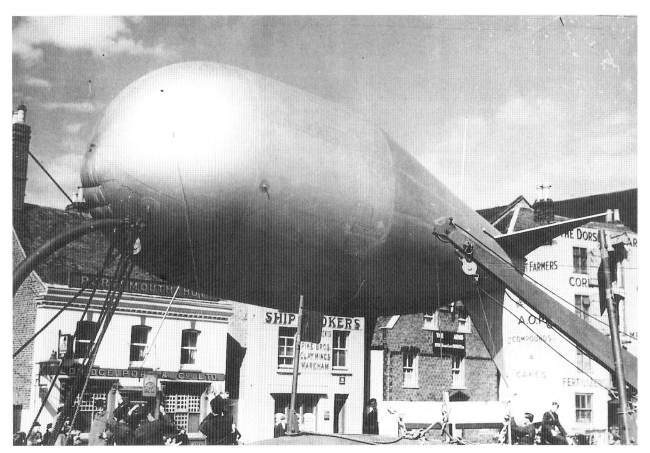

A Barrage Balloon suspended over Poole Quay and photographed from a minesweeper moored opposite the Portsmouth Hoy.

(Top) General Officer Commanding Royal Marines, takes the salute as the crews of the Landing Craft Support Squadron from HMS Turtle, march past along Lake Drive, Hamworthy in May 1944.

(Centre) The crews of the Landing Craft Support Squadron on parade at HMS Turtle in May 1944. In the background is a representative collection of the Squadron's craft.

(Left) Troops from the US Army Transportation Corps (14 Port Sub-Port) on Poole Quay in 1944.

ALL CRAFT WILL PROCEED TO POINT X RAY

Once the loading of the convoys had been completed a hush fell over the harbour and quayside. Many Poole people who had seen the frantic activity of the last days of May and early June thought it might all be just another exercise, but they wondered. Those who looked out on Poole Bay on Sunday 4th June had fewer doubts that the long awaited invasion was at hand. The Bay was filling with ships while destroyers guarded the approaches to the coast. Convoys of landing craft came up from the west and anchored in Studland Bay. As the day wore on larger ships came into the Bay The first was a warship towed in with difficulty by a tug. She was the old French battleship *COURBET*, destined to be sunk as a breakwater off the invasion coast to provide a makeshift harbour. Presently she was joined by some 3 other obsolete warships and, over the next day, by 58 old tramp ships (23 of them American) which had all managed the journey from Scotland under their own steam. This odd fleet, codenamed *CORNCOBS*, had left Oban six days earlier, and were destined to a final journey of self immolation on the beaches of the 'far shore'.

But the weather was growing worse. A surging wind brought white capped waves and buffeted the craft tossing at their anchors in the bay. From time to time they were lost to sight in squalls of rain. Those watching from the cliffs were not to know that this rising storm had caused Eisenhower and the Allied Commanders to postpone D-Day for 24 hours, requiring the recall of some of the slower craft that had by then set sail. In the clearing weather of Monday there was an even grander spectacle. Convoy after convoy came up from beyond Old Harry Rocks and headed for the assembly area, Point X Ray, south of the Isle of Wight, referred to as 'Piccadilly Circus'. They were joined by another long line of craft steaming out of Poole Harbour, put in order by the navigation leaders, although in the event only one of the R.A.F. dispatch boats was operational and the U.S. Coastguard cutters had to substitute. Out on the horizon, a procession of heavy warships, battleships and cruisers could be glimpsed through the shifting mist. Overhead were swarms of watchful fighters.

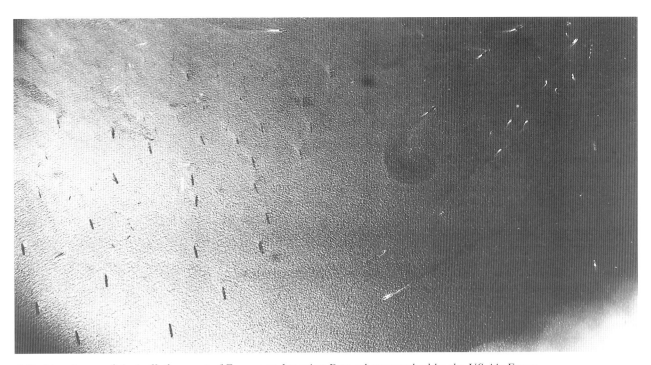

Allied landing craft just off the coast of France on Invasion Day, photographed by the US Air Force.

5th PARACHUTE BRIGADE WILL SEIZE THE CROSSINGS OVER THE RIVER AND CANAL

Not everyone had heard about, or seen what was happening out in the Bay. War-time life was hard and comparatively few had time or the inclination to take cliff-top walks. It was the thunder of the aircraft crossing on the night of 5th June which made everyone guess that the invasion was starting. Squadron after squadron of bombers, many towing gliders, were taking British and American parachute and glider-borne troops to begin the assault . Quite unusually they were flying with their navigation lights on and some of them could be seen in breaks amongst the clouds. Two of these squadrons, Nos. 298 and 644 had taken off from Tarrant Rushton, just north of Wimborne. Six of these aircraft released their gliders just before midnight over the Caen canal where the Oxford and Bucks Light Infantry seized two vital bridges. They were followed over France by another 17 aircraft and gliders from Tarrant Rushton.

ALLIED NAVAL FORCES BEGAN LANDING ALLIED ARMIES THIS MORNING...

Before the night was out military convoys began to move along the roads again. People going to work found their buses delayed by long columns of tanks, guns and D.U.K.W.S. as the follow-up forces moved to the coast. Finally, at 9.33am General Eisenhower's announcement that the invasion had started put an end to all rumours. In homes and factories there was a pause in work while everyone digested the momentous news, many thinking of relatives and friends in the forces who were bound to be part of this hazardous venture. Churches and chapels opened for private prayer and special services. Those who saw Poole Harbour were amazed at how empty it appeared. Mothers with young children took them to watch the continuing procession of craft passing through Poole Bay, telling them they would never see such a spectacle again.

TROOPS WERE LANDED UNDER CONSIDERABLE ENEMY FIRE...

The assault convoy from Poole battled its way across the Channel on 5th June. Heavy weather and strong currents meant that those vessels towing other landing craft were always in danger of falling behind or going off course. Despite this, the bulk of the convoy arrived off Omaha Beach on time. Promptly at 5.50am on 6th June the American battleships and British cruisers opened fire on the defences. As this ceased. Captain Sabin's gun craft on the flanks of the assault strained to pick out their targets amidst the smoke and dust raised by the bombardment. The rocket craft released 79 tons of missiles onto the beach. But by now the unexpectedly high waves and surf were taking their toll. Many of the 'swimming' tanks and D.U.K.W.S. were swamped as soon as they were launched.

As the demolition teams and infantry neared the shore, enemy guns opened up, sinking many of the craft. Machine gun and mortar fire cut across the beach, killing or wounding many of those troops who scrambled ashore. For some hours the result of the battle hung in the balance. But gradually the sheer determination

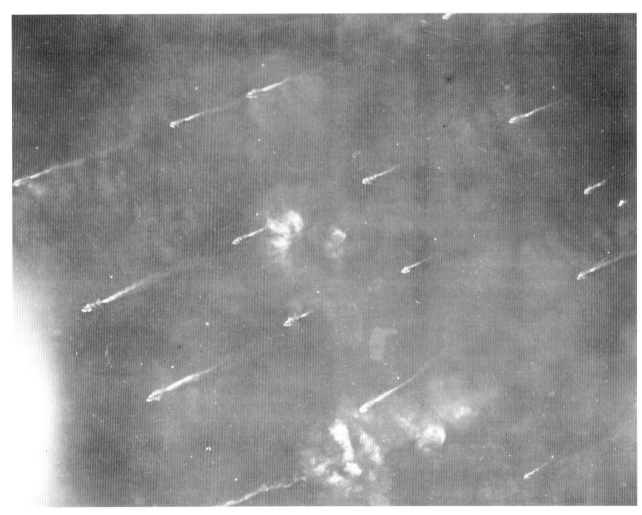

The four long columns of craft steered out into the Channel.

An early version of the British Power Boat 68' Target Towing Launch at speed in Poole Bay.

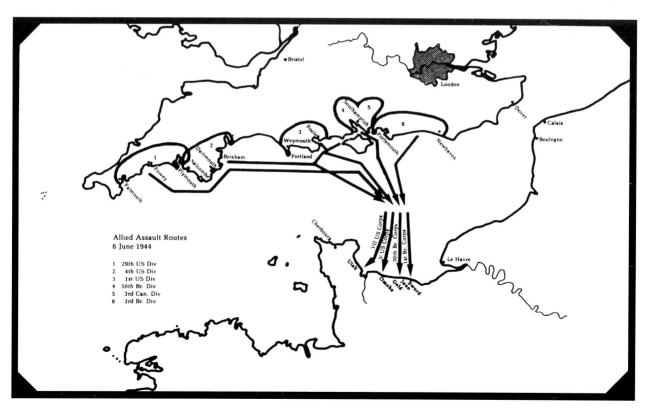

Plan of the Allied Assault Routes on Normandy, 6 June 1944.

(Above) The aftermath of battle on Omaha Beach shortly after the US forces had fought their way inland against terrifying opposition from the defending German troops.

(Left) US personnel crossing the English Channel from Poole to Omaha Beach, 5 June 1944 (D-Day Minus One).

ALL FORCE G UNITS WILL MOVE...

Up until January 1944 Poole was to be one of the main bases for the British invasion forces. Force G, assaulting Gold Beach, was to be launched from the Dorset ports. Then, when Montgomery insisted that the invasion front should be widened, the main facilities in Poole were allocated to the American troops who would attack over the Omaha and Utah beaches. But Force G, including the 1st Battalion of the Dorsetshire Regiment, the East Yorkshire and the Green Howards, needed to stay as long as possible in the Poole area to make use of the battle practice grounds there. They did not leave until 1944.

Veterans of another unit, the 86 Field Regiment, Hertfordshire Yeomanry, R.A., remember their days in Poole very clearly. Leaving their tented camps in Hamworthy Park and Rockley, they drove their Ram self-propelled guns onto tank landing craft at *HMS Turtle*. Sweeping out into Studland Bay, they turned for the beach, firing their 25 pounders as they stormed in to cover the landing of the troops. Other exercises used Brownsea Island and at least one steel helmet accidentally dropped into the water must still lie in the Harbour mud! After these last rehearsals 86 Regiment took their guns to the Alumhurst Road district in Bournemouth. Here they waterproofed their equipment before moving off to a sealed camp in woods near Romsey, waiting for their journey to Southampton and Normandy.

UNITED STATES FORCES ARE READY TO DEPLOY IN THE POOLE AREA...

Well before the British troops left, the Americans moved in. The U.S. Infantry 1st Division set up its headquarters under General Bradley in Langton House, near Blandford, in October 1943. 'The Fighting First', known as the 'Big Red One' from its distinctive badge, included many veterans of the landings in North Africa and Sicily. They were to be joined in the battle for Omaha Beach by men of the U.S. 29th Division, the 'Blue and Grey' and the 2nd and 5th Ranger Battalions, the American Commandos. These troops moved into tented camps in the Dorchester area. Another American force took over the fine Elizabethan mansion at Breamore. General Patton was to make it his headquarters.

The Americans soon made their mark on Poole and the surrounding district. Their engineers built 22nd General Hospital at Blandford and a large petrol depot at West Moors. Two more hospitals went up at St. Leonards, near Ringwood, to cater for up to 10,000 expected casualties, and at Shaftesbury. The 2nd Ranger Battalion who had the difficult task of scaling the 100 feet high cliffs at Pointe du Hoc to destroy a menacing battery of 6 German guns, moved into Langton Matravers. They rehearsed by climbing the cliffs at Swanage from their British assault craft. The 58th Army Field Artillery Battalion moved into Charborough Park (where, incidentally, the Borough Archives had been moved for safety and suffered more damage from damp and vermin than in the previous 500 years).

More and more GI's moved into Poole, taking over requisitioned halls, hotels and private

of the few surviving officers and non-commissioned officers and the equal valour of the GI's carried the day. They were backed by the gun craft and destroyers which came in so close to the beach to hammer home their attack that they were in danger of grounding. One by one the enemy strongpoints were silenced and small groups of troops were able to climb the low cliffs. By 8.00pm on the evening of D-Day the beaches and cliffs had been wrested from the grip of the enemy although only two of 16 planned gaps had been created. Over three thousand young Americans had been killed or wounded... over half the men of the demolition team...two thirds of 'A' Company of the 29th Division's 116th Infantry Regiment.

The Rangers fought just as fierce a battle for Pointe du Hoc. Suffering heavy casualties, they found the gun emplacement at the top of the cliffs empty. Undeterred, they moved inland to discover the heavy guns standing ready to be mounted. Having blown them up, they fought on against heavy odds until help reached them from 1st Division troops .

Elsewhere the landings, although hard, were less bloody. *HMS Poole* was amongst the minesweepers which cleared the way for the attack of Utah Beach. The 1st Dorsets and 1st Hampshires were the first British troops ashore in Normandy. With them in the 50th Division landing on Gold Beach were other units which had come to know Poole. The men of the 86 Field Regiment R.A. felt that their landing craft were in danger of shaking apart from the recoil of their 25 pounders as they fired at the beach defences on their run-in to the shore at La Riviere. A specially equipped tank flailed the ground ahead of them to destroy enemy mines as their guns ground their way across the beach to seek more targets. Close by them, on Juno Beach, the 3rd Canadian Infantry Division were fighting hard against determined opposition which was to cost them 1,000 casualties that day. On Sword Beach, the men of the 1st Royal Marine Support Craft Battery were no strangers to Poole either. They had taken part in many exercises from Poole and were now firing at a live enemy in Ouistreham instead of the empty beach at Studland.

HMS Poole, a minesweeper of the Bangor Class moored at Poole Quay

TURN ROUND CONTROL AND FERRY ORDERS FOLLOW:

The initial success of the Allied landings was far from meaning that Poole's role in the invasion had come to an end. Returning landing craft brought casualties and survivors. Many craft needed repair - all of them needed to replenish their fuel, ammunition and rations. To make sure that the beachheads were expanded many more men and supplies had to be brought in using Mulberry harbours. As if to remind local people of the dangers of war a Liberator had crashed near Furzey Island on 6th June and burnt out. There were no survivors.

On 8th June, the American rocket firing craft returned to Poole from Omaha to unload wounded men and survivors. Soon afterwards the first British craft put in from Utah Beach. *HMS Turtle* received 250 survivors from them. Some of the 1,400 Allied troops and 1 German airman rescued by the Coastguard cutters also returned to Poole. The Flotilla's own ambulances took the wounded amongst them to the American hospitals nearby. In the 6 weeks after D-Day nearly 900 craft were re-fuelled and re-stocked in the harbour. In the same period an average of 15 landing craft each week were repaired by the bases in the port. Bolson's took in some of the heavily damaged vessels.

In September 1944 the flying boat services, suspended since April, resumed their use of the Harbour. From August the public were able to use the beaches again – though they were still used by the military forces.

Meanwhile the ferry service to run supplies to Normandy began its work in Poole. By the end of the year about 1,000 merchant made movements had taken place from Poole - a gross tonnage of 300,000. Working in 48 hour shifts, the crews of the landing craft and tankers shuttled to and from the beachheads. None of the craft was allowed to stay in the harbour longer than was required to re-fuel and re-load for the 'far shore'. The R.N. crews snatched baths and brief rests in bunks installed in the hotels at Sandbanks between trips. They kept this pace up until April 1945. By then they had delivered 56,000,000 gallons of fuel and tons of ammunition and rations to Normandy. Once this service was ended the U.S. Transportation Corps left the town, E.N.S.A. visits ceased and it was once again possible for Poole people to walk along the Quay.

The U.S. Navy had left long before - in August 1944 - too soon to enjoy the American Red Cross Club, incorporating a bath house, which opened that month in Poole's old Guildhall. In the last stages of the war it was thus the Royal Navy and the Royal Marines who made most use of the harbour. It was from Poole that the 25 craft of the Royal Marine Support Squadron sailed to cover the assault on Walcheren in November 1944. Until the enemy had been defeated there, the great port of Antwerp was useless to the Allies and without it they could not hope to roll back the enemy any further. Despite intense enemy fire, which sank 9 of their craft and crippled another 9, the Royal Marines from *HMS Turtle* pressed home their attack. Walcheren fell and Antwerp was opened to a flood of allied reinforcements.

(Top right) US Coast Guard Cutters of No.1 Rescue Flotilla in dry dock at Poole in August 1944.

(Bottom right) VE Day in Poole, the gun-craft of the Support Squadron from HMS Turtle are dressed overall in honour of this great occasion.

Official U.S. records state of the Poole operations that "the finest co-operation and the best spirit of co-operation prevailed" and this accolade is still cherished in Poole although, fifty years on, the town and the harbour have changed in appearance dramatically. Much that was familiar to the servicemen and residents of 1944 has disappeared, but enough remains to re-awaken memories of that time. The Nissen hut near Poole Bridge which was part of Poole Naval Centre is still remembered by many and the Centre's headquarters building in the Cornmarket in High Street now stands empty. So does the old Guildhall. The building where many Poole children shared doughnuts with the American servicemen is now awaiting a new use. St James' Church still houses the United States ensign used by the U.S. Coastguard Flotilla based in Poole. Carters (Poole) Pottery was rebuilt soon after the war but despite this and other changes it is still possible to visualise the Coastguard cutters moored by the Quay and the bustle of landing craft loading along the quayside up to the Fishermen's Dock. Beyond here, the area of Baiter, where ammunition was stored and A.A. guns were sited, has changed almost beyond recognition, but the remains of the ancient gunpowder store, also used in the war, remain on the shore.

On the wall of the former Custom House on the Quay a plaque was unveiled in 1984 to record Poole's part in Operation Overlord. Part of Slade's warehouse remains but has now been redeveloped as high class housing and renamed Barber's Quay.

At Hamworthy two veteran landing craft still serve as a breakwater off the quay. Bolson's shipyard is still busy. Through the security fencing around the Royal Marine's Amphibious Warfare Centre in Lake Road the passer-by can discern the tank 'hard' of *HMS Turtle*, now dealing with modern landing craft. The houses and bungalows nearby are still recognisable as the requisitioned properties that once rang with the naval commands in British and American accents. The gallantry of the Royal Marines at Walcheren is fittingly commemorated in Hamworthy Church.

Land reclamation has changed the shape of Poole Harbour. Cross channel passenger ferries now carry goods of peace and yachts ride at moorings where once landing craft lay waiting. But in the names of the channels and reaches of the Harbour are those which appear in the invasion orders. Standing at Evening Hill or North Haven Point, it takes little imagination to see once again the processions of landing craft moving past Aunt Betty Buoy and Brownsea Island to the Swash Channel and the open sea.

For many who live in Poole or visit the town the 50th anniversary of D-Day will regrettably be a sad time - others too will remember the memorial notices in local newspapers for those of the British, Canadian and American forces who sacrificed their lives. But all can be proud of the achievements of those men and the veterans who live on. We can also take humble pride in what Poole contributed to the common cause on D-Day.